Sail on the Mers

by
Michael Stammers

Acknowledgements

I would like to thank the following for allowing the use of their photographs:— Liverpool City Engineers, a Mersey Flat, page 25; Keith Lewis, The Nantucket, page 4; Dr. D. Chapman, Topsail schooner, outward bound, page 12; K. Kortum, San Francisco Maritime Museum, two views of the Jhelum, page 19; Peter Throckmorton, Elissa, page 27; Dick Scott, De Wadden at Widnes Dock, page 31; J.H. Williams, A.R.P.S., Hoylake Trawlers in Albert Dock, page 33; Ron Jones, Boys and their Boats, page 36; D.E. Smith, A.R.P.S., Bengullion in the Mersey, inside back cover; and the Merseyside Maritime Museum from whose collections the rest of the pictures have been taken.

I would also like to thank my wife for all her work and encouragement.

Frontispiece:
Topsail schooner outward bound off Birkenhead.

Facing Page:
Queens Dock one hundred years ago, looking north to Wapping and Salthouse Docks with a dozen deep sea sailing ships loading cargoes.

Following Pages:
1. The American three masted barque Nantucket *berthed in the Albert Dock in June 1934, one of many foreign sail training vessels that have visited the port since the 1920s.*

2. Sail training today, the modern fibre glass ketches of the Ocean Youth Club sail past the Merseyside Maritime Museum on its opening day in 1980. The O.Y.C.'s Francis Drake is a frequent visitor to the Mersey.

First published 1984 by Countyvise Limited, 1 & 3 Grove Road, Rock Ferry, Birkenhead, Wirral, Merseyside L42 3XS.
ISBN 0 907768 85 7

Copyright © Michael Stammers, 1984.
Photoset and printed by Birkenhead Press Limited, 1 & 3 Grove Road, Rock Ferry, Birkenhead, Wirral, Merseyside L42 3XS.

Introduction

One hundred years ago the Mersey was crowded with sailing ships. The tall masts of deep sea barques and ships were to be seen in almost every dock. The picture of Queens Dock in the 1880s was typical. Hundreds of small craft, flats, schooners, gig boats, fishing trawlers, all worked under sail. Many of the growing fleet of steamers still carried full sets of sails as a sort of 'belt and braces' precaution in case their engines broke down.

This publication illustrates the history of sailing ships on the Mersey over the last one hundred and fifty years. It has views of the river and the docks in the days of sail and pictures of some of the different types of vessel to be seen. It also has pictures of some of the most famous ships of the sailing ship era including the most famous of them all, the tea clipper *Cutty Sark*.

There was a rapid decline in sailing ships using and owned in the port in the first two decades of our century. The Liverpool owned sailing ship fleets which had once been large and powerful organisations were nearly all dispersed by about 1910 because of the continuing depression in the freight rates for the bulk cargoes such as coal and grain by which they paid their way. Ocean going sailing ships usually under the Finnish flag continued to arrive with cargoes of grain right up until the Second World War. But they came as single ships and their rarity created great local interest. A new type of deep sea sailing ship also began to be seen in the Mersey — the sail training ship. Apart from the White Star Lines pioneer effort with their officer cadet ship *Mersey* before 1914 all these ships flew foreign flags — Norwegian, German, American etc.; for instance the American barque *Nantucket* called in 1934 and was berthed in the Albert Dock. British interest in sail training (now for young people and not for potential seamen) revived in the 1960s. The graceful schooners *Malcolm Miller* and *Sir Winston Churchill* belonging to the Sail Training Association, the Sea Cadet's brig *Royalist* and the Ocean Youth Clubs big ketch *Francis Drake* have all been seen on the Mersey in recent years and there have also been visits by Thames barges, schooners like the *Charlotte Rhodes* of Onedin Line fame and the China Clipper Society's two square riggers *Marques* and *Inca*. So the sail has never entirely vanished from the Mersey and 1984 will bring the biggest sailing ship fleet since the turn of the century when the Tall Ships fleet of over sixty ships dock at Albert Dock and Birkenhead.

The *Marco Polo* in the River Mersey

The *Marco Polo* is the most celebrated of all the Liverpool sailing ships. She was owned by the Liverpool Black Ball Line and was the first ship to substantially shorten the voyage time from England to Australia.

She was built in Marsh Creek near St. John, New Brunswick, Canada and launched in 1851. She was built of wood and measured 185 feet long, 35 feet in the beam, 29 feet depth of hold with a tonnage of 1625 tons. This made her a very large ship indeed for her time. The average size of ship owned in Liverpool was no more than five to six hundred tons.

Like many Canadian ships of the mid 19th century she was built as a speculation to be sent over to Liverpool for sale. Canadian ships found a ready market here because they were markedly cheaper than the locally built ships. However it was claimed that the Canadian ships were badly built, badly designed and constructed from poor materials. Like many generalisations this one tends to break down when you look at individual cases. While it is true that the *Marco Polo* was built of Canadian pine, oak and other woods rated as being of inferior strength to good English oak she nevertheless lasted a considerable time — 32 years in fact. Her hull design owed much to the American packet ships which were amongst the fastest most seaworthy ships of their time and certainly there were few if any British shipbuilders who could build such a large ship so well and so cheaply as James Smith, the *Marco Polo's* builder. Possibly her worst feature was her very deep draught. This made it difficult for her to leave or enter the Liverpool docks fully loaded except on Spring tides.

James Smith sent her to Liverpool in 1851 with a cargo of timber but failed to find a buyer for her. From the small number of new entries in the second half of 1851 it seems as if the ship market was at a fairly low level. So, Smith loaded her with a cargo for Mobile where he was able to find a return cargo of cotton for Liverpool. She was again put up for sale and this time she was bought by James

Baines and Company. She was fitted out to carry passengers and cargo to Australia. She caused something of a stir even then for her picture was drawn for the leading illustrated magazine of the time (that is the picture in this book) and a comprehensive report of her features and fittings published. The report mentions the excellence of her construction;

> '*In strength she could not well be excelled. Her timbering is enormous*' and the choice decoration of the first class accommodation; '*On deck forward of the poop is a 'home on deck' to be used as a dining saloon. It is ceiled with maple and the pilasters are panelled with richly ornamented silvered glass – coins of various countries being a novel feature of the decoration.*'

She was ready to sail in July 1852 with no less than 950 passengers aboard. Australia was an exceedingly popular destination because of the discovery of gold in New South Wales the previous year. Liverpool ship owners were quick to seize the chance to carry gold diggers and cargo out to the Gold Rush. The Australian trade had been something of a monopoly of the port of London in previous years. The problem of going to Australia was the time it took — 120 days if you were lucky. There was no Suez canal and it was a case of having to sail right the way round the bottom end of Africa — the Cape of Good Hope. The *Marco Polo* made her first voyage out in only 76 days and made the entire round trip in 5 months and 21 days — an astonishing performance which attracted much publicity and passengers for the Black Ball Line. Her record was partly due to her design and size and partly due to her remarkable commander Captain James Forbes, popularly known as Bully Forbes. Bully Forbes was a strict

A stern carving from the 'Marco Polo'.

disciplinarian who drove his ship and his crew. He was also an excellent navigator who was prepared to try a new course to Australia which involved taking his ship way to the South of the Cape of Good Hope to the strong but constant winds of the Roaring Forties. In doing so and by constantly keeping his ship under the most possible sail he was able to make some very fast voyages. He and his ship made the reputation of the Line which grew and prospered. The *Marco Polo* continued to carry passengers for the Line until 1867. Curiously she made her last outward trip in 76 days Liverpool to Melbourne — the same as her record breaking first passage. After that she was used for more general cargo carrying and sold to South Shields owners in 1871. She was used to carry bulk cargoes such as coal and timber. In 1883 after several changes of ownership she left Quebec with a cargo of timber. Unfortunately she sprang a bad leak and her captain decided to beach her on the shore of Prince Edward Island in order to save her. A gale arose before she could be repaired and refloated and she was broken up were she lay. Many souvenirs of this famous old ship were rescued by the local farmers. These included the famous stern carvings showing the Venetian explorer in Eastern and Western dress and a carving of an elephant. The Maritime Museum is very fortunate to have two accurate copies of the figures of Marco Polo and in time we hope to have one of the elephant as well and this is why I have made a sketch of him.

Salthouse Dock in the 1880s

The crowded port, Salthouse Dock packed with square riggers. Four vessels are visible just in the north east corner of the dock. The Salthouse Dock was the second dock built in Liverpool. It was started in 1738 and completed in 1753 and it took its name from the salt refinery which stood on the site of the dock. Salt was a major export from Liverpool both in the 18th and 19th century. By the time of this photograph the salt was all processed in Cheshire and was carried down the Weaver and the Mersey in barges (flats). A flat can be seen in the foreground tied up alongside a three masted barque. She has unloaded her cargo and rides high out of the water. Originally all flats were sailing craft. By the last quarter of the 19th century many were cut down to dumb barges and towed by tugs and Weaver steam packets. The barque herself has almost finished loading her cargo and on deck work is under way to get ready for sea and the sails have been roused out of the sail locker and sent aloft. Behind the barque is an unknown white hulled full rigged ship possibly one of Thompson Anderson's famous Sierra Line and the iron ship *Atlantic*.

The finely carved figurehead in toga, tunic and sandals amidst the bowsprit rigging belongs to another square rigger moored along the north quay of Salthouse Dock. The ships of the sailing era were built as individual vessels. Not many were standard designs. This individuality was expressed in all sorts of ways from hull shape to height of masts. One of the most striking for almost all these ships and unique to each one was her figurehead or bow decoration. The graceful 'clipper' bow lent itself to such ornament.

The carved figures, many of which were executed in the workshops of Liverpool's ship carvers, came in a whole variety of forms. Often they might be a human figure which reflected the name of the ship; no doubt in this case it was a hero of Classical mythology. Others carried the portraits of their owners or perhaps their wives or daughters. Docks like the Salthouse were colourful outdoor sculpture galleries with all those ships's figureheads.

The other intriguing aspect of this picture is just how large the latter day square riggers were. All the ships in the picture were about 200 feet long, masts reaching up to over 150 feet and carrying up to 2000 tons of cargo. This is quite a jump from the ships for which the Salthouse Dock was opened — little wooden ships of less than 100 foot, carrying 200 tons. Yet these little ships carried Liverpool's deep sea trade to the West Indies, North America, West Africa and the Baltic. The sketch of one of these little ships is drawn from a ship illustrated on a plan of the Liverpool docks in 1765.

Topsail Schooner, Outward Bound

Fair wind, outward bound, a topsail schooner has most of her sails hoisted to run before the light but favourable wind to carry her out of the Mersey. She has probably set sail from the Sloyne anchorage off Tranmere. This was much used by the little sailing coasters bound for the upper Mersey ports of Runcorn, Weston Point, Widnes and Ellesmere Port. From Tranmere they would be towed up the narrow, ever changing deep channel of the upper estuary by a tug. One of the main cargoes was china clay from Cornwall and Devon for the Staffordshire potteries. This was transhipped into canal boats at Runcorn or one of the other ports mentioned for the final leg of its journey to Staffordshire. Many of the 'china clay' schooners loaded coal as a return cargo.

This particular schooner was probably photographed off Liverpool about 1900. By then she was quite a vintage vessel for her rig has an old fashioned look about it with her separate bowsprit and jib boom, her narrow, deep topsails and that splendid jackyard main top topsail. It is a pity that she has not as yet been identified.

A sizeable fleet of schooners continued to work into the Mersey until the Second World War. But competition from motor lorries and motor coasters and old age saw a gradual thinning out. The great depression in trade from 1929 did not help either. After the First World War many were fitted with auxiliary engines. The results were mixed, many of the older skippers disliked these smelly mechanical contraptions and as a result engines were misunderstood, misused and badly maintained. However the technical improvements in the diesel engines themselves greatly improved their reliability and by the mid thirties there were only a handful of schooners trading under sail alone. Their main cargoes were china clay, stone and timber. They were often to be seen unloading not only at Runcorn but also at the stone berth in the Canning Half Tide Dock — now a part of the Merseyside Maritime Museum.

At Runcorn, Grounds & Co. ran the last fleet of sailing ships owned on the Mersey into the 1930s. They included the *Fanny Crossfield, J.H. Barrow, Mary Miller, Mary Sinclair, Shoal Fisher, Gauntlet, Bidsie and Bell* and *Mary Wilkinson*. One by one all had disappeared by the Second World War. The *Shoal Fisher* went down in the Bay of Biscay after a collision in 1932 for example. The *Mary Sinclair* was seriously damaged in the Mersey in 1936 and was sold to Abels of Widnes as a sand barge. All her masts and spars and most of her deck were removed and she was towed from the dredger to the dock by a tug. She continued in this sand carrying work until finally broken up shortly after the Second World War.

The *Oak*

A vintage sailing vessel that survived to the early part of this century was the *Oak*. She was built for the Dock Surveyor Jesse Hartley in 1836 for carrying granite from the quarries at Kirkmabreck on the Scottish side of the Solway Firth for building docks and dock buildings at Liverpool. Hartley, who was dock engineer or surveyor to give him his proper title, was responsible for the Liverpool docks between 1824 and his death in 1860. He transformed the port. To cope with the ever growing number of ships sailing to the Mersey he doubled the number of docks and built many new facilities such as the great warehouses at Albert, Stanley and Wapping Docks to receive the high value cargoes such as tobacco, cotton, wines and spirits; he linked the important Leeds and Liverpool canal to the rest of the docks and much more besides. Many of his works are still standing including the famous Albert Dock which is being transformed into an attractive new amenity with the Maritime Museum, shops, restaurants, flats and offices in Hartley's wonderful warehouses. All his work witnessed his passion for that most durable of buildings stones — granite. The *Oak* and a flotilla of other little ships transported huge quantities of the stone for building dock and river walls and buildings. The *Oak* was as stout as her name for she survived in this hard stone carrying business until the turn of the century and even then she was sold for further trading and not for breaking up.

Fruit Schooners in Georges Dock 1880

In Victorian times Georges Dock was the centre of the imported fruit trade. It was a seasonal business starting about October and finishing in the following Spring. By the 1850s over 15,000 tons of oranges, lemons and grapes were brought to Liverpool, mainly in small but very fast schooners from the Mediterranean and the Azores. The St. Michael's oranges from the Azores were especially in demand. Of course the carriage of these perishable fruits was eventually taken over by steamers which could offer a much more reliable delivery. But there were still fruit schooners sailing to Liverpool as late as the 1880s. In the north east corner of the dock close by the Tower Building (an office block which once had a semaphore signal station on its tower) and St. Nicholas Church lie three schooners and a brigantine. In front of the brigantine is a steam launch (purpose unknown) and the salvage steamer of the Liverpool Salvage Association. The sails are raised not for departing the dock but to dry out the canvas.

Georges Dock was first opened in 1771, the third dock of the port and was closed in 1899. Today, the Mersey Docks and Harbour Co. offices and the Cunard Building stand on its site.

Fruit schooners carried a lot of sail for speed and the sketch shows one carrying a square foresail, two topsails and a topgallant in her last burst of speed to reach Georges Dock with her ripening cargo.

Gigboats

Gigboats were used to assist ships into the Mersey and the docks. They were especially useful for passing heavy ropes between the ship and the quay for warping (i.e. moving the ship) or mooring. They might also carry out passengers, crew or ship's agents and supplies to ships at anchor in the river. Competition was keen in the days of sail and they often went as far as Holyhead in their quest for inward bound ships. Some of their number were rather notorious because they would offer to deputise for members of the crew of a homeward bounder who were desperate to get ashore to taste the joys of Liverpool. They were duly taken ashore to some cheap boarding house cum pub and charged steep prices for board, lodging and drink. Within a very few days all the hard earned wages would have been mopped up by their spree and they were quickly shipped out again to the profit of their hosts.

The gigboats were heavily built open boats rigged with two, and in fair weather three, masts. They carried spritsails which could be easily furled. They could also be easily rowed. This picture shows a race for gigboats. For many years they were a feature of the Royal Mersey Sailing Club regatta with the prizes being donated by a well known local brewery.

Many of the boats were based on the old Chester Basin which was filled in about 1930 and now lies under the patch of grass in front of the Maritime Museum car park. With an antique hand crane the gigboatmen would lift out their boats for painting and repair. When in service many were moored behind the old Liverpool Landing Stage. The sailing boats had more or less faded out by the 1920s and certainly the old ways of seeking sailing ships as far out as North Wales had gone out with the steep decline in sailing ships using the port in the early 1900s. Small reliable diesel engines were available and the new boats were designed for power and not for rowing or sailing. They were carvel and not clinker built and larger than their predecessors. Unfortunately all the old sailing gigboats seem to have disappeared. There are none left to preserve, but the Maritime Museum does have a fine model of a sailing boat together with the full size motor gigboat the *Elizabeth*.

Cutty Sark
in the West Float, Birkenhead, 1914.

The *Cutty Sark* is the best known of all British deep sea sailing ships. She was built on the Clyde at Dumbarton in 1869. She was of composite build with iron frames and wooden planking and was intended to beat the best ships in the China tea trade. At the time of her launch sailing ships still dominated this premium trade racing home from Shanghai and Foo Chow to be first home to the Thames with the new crop of tea, both for the prestige and for a substantial bonus on the freight money. The opening of the Suez Canal in 1869 and the progress in compound marine steam engines meant that the tea clippers were pushed out of their dominant position in the next decade. The pioneer line in the Far East steamship business was Liverpool's Blue Funnel Line which began a service to Hong Kong with economical compound engined steamers in 1866.

By 1877, as a result of the steamers, the *Cutty Sark* was transferred to the Australian wool trade and she still continued to make fast voyages. Eventually she could not be made to pay in this trade and in 1895 she was sold to Portugese owners who renamed her *Ferreira* but even though she had a new name there was no disguising her origins; her fine lines and splendid fittings gave her away. So she attracted the interest of many people whenever she returned to a British port. In 1914 and 1915 she delivered two cargoes of whale oil from West Africa to Birkenhead and on the first occasion an unknown local photographer took this historic picture. In 1916 she was dismasted and her lofty ship rig was reduced to that of a barquentine.

When she visited London in 1922 her arrival caused much interest. Captain Wilfred Dowman, an ex-sailing ship man, decided that she ought to be preserved. He bought her, re-rigged her and kept her in Falmouth. Eventually she went to the Thames to become part of the training facilities of *H.M.S. Worcester*, the school ship and finally in the early 1950s she was completely restored to her condition as a tea clipper and placed for permanent preservation in a special dry dock at Greenwich on the Thames where she can still be seen today.

The techniques of sailing big square riggers like the *Cutty Sark* are carried on by the training ships which compete in the Tall Ships Races. The principal prize is very aptly called the Cutty Sark Trophy. It is a silver model of this famous old tea clipper.

Most of the tea clippers were owned in London including the *Cutty Sark* and virtually all the tea was taken to the Thames as well. But a number of tea clippers were built at Liverpool including the two *Fiery Crosses* one of 1858 and one of 1860 and there were also a handful owned here as well. These included Beazley's *Vision* of 1854 of which there is a painting and a model in the collections of the Maritime Museum and Rathbone's *Scawfell* of 1858.

Ready To Leave
A three masted barque about to leave Canning Half Tide Dock

Ready to leave, a British three masted barque prepares to move out of the Canning Half Tide Dock entrance into the River Mersey outward bound. This quay, now put back to its 19th century appearance, is part of the Merseyside Maritime Museum. In the days of the sailing ships it was the place for many a 'pier head jump'. It seems that quite often members of the crew, having signed on, would go off just before the sailing time for one last drink or two. Some did not make it back to the ship. By the time the ship had been moved to the Canning Half Tide Dock entrance her officers would have given them up as lost and would get last minute replacements from the little group of unemployed seamen who gathered in the hope of doing the 'pier head jump'.

The gentlemen in the cap and smart uniform coat was the piermaster. He controlled the movement of ships in and out of the docks and allocated their berths. He was helped by a team of dock gatemen who opened and closed the lock gates and bridges to let the vessels pass. His job was an arduous one because he was expected to attend the opening and closing of the gates into the river before and after each high tide. As a result piermasters at Canning and at the other river entrances were provided with a house right on the waterfront by the Dock Board. The house for the piermaster in the picture has survived in crumbling condition, derelict and untenanted for over the last thirty years. Now, it has been rebuilt and restored to its appearance in the early 1900s.

The strange 'Dalek' structure on the side of the ship is a light tower to raise the starboard navigation light well above the waterline to make it more visible to other ships. There was a similar light tower on the port side. The black shed in the background was used for storing curb and paving stones unloaded from coasting schooners and next to it there is a steam coaster in Canning Number Two Graving Dock.

The *Jhelum*

The *Jhelum* was built in the South Docks of Liverpool in 1849. She was a wooden three masted ship of just over 400 tons and was a 127 feet long. As such she was typical of the ships being built in the port in the mid 19th century — very small compared to the great iron and steel sailing ships of the second part of the century. Her unusual name comes from a river in India. It is probably because of this that she has often been described as an East Indiaman. In fact this is not true; she made just one voyage to India, her first. Then she traded to South America. One of her main cargoes was guano, a noisome cargo. It was the bird droppings from the millions of sea birds found along the coast and islands of Peru, especially the Chincha Islands. There were millions of tons and when it was discovered in the 1840s that it made a very useful fertilizer it was shipped in large quantities to European ports.

The *Jhelum* was carrying a cargo of guano on her last voyage in 1870. She was sailing from the West coast of South America round Cape Horn bound for the French port of Dunkirk. She sprang a leak perhaps because of the corrosive chemicals in the guano and was obliged to put into the nearest port of refuge, Port Stanley in the Falkland Islands. After much wrangling it turned out that her owners had neither the money to pay for the repairs or her crew. She was therefore abandoned. The resourceful Falkland islanders beached her on the edge of Stanley harbour and built a jetty out to her, turning her into a cheap unloading berth and warehouse. Her masts were cut off and her upper deck roofed over so that she looked a bit like Noah's Ark. Her abandonment in the Falklands has ensured her survival. Although she has now no longer any use as a store hulk she still survives and as such is a unique example of a Liverpool built deep sea wooden sailing ship.

Whether she will remain in her present condition is open to question. The Falklands do not have the resources to preserve her and her old timbers are giving way as wind, rain and sea take their toll. The deterioration has increased since the Falklands War because of all the extra ships using the harbour.

Under the section preserved by the corrugated roof at her stern end the timbers, great baulks of English oak and African mahogany, are in very good condition. The workmanship of them with their fancy mouldings is a fine testament to the quality of work produced by the Liverpool shipwrights of the 1840s. Colonel John Blashford-Snell's world-wide expedition for young people (Operation Raleigh) plans to visit the Falklands to work on the historic shipwrecks there. I hope they will include the *Jhelum* in their programme.

The Last of the Sailing Ships

By the 1890s it was increasingly clear that the time of the sailing ship even in the low cost bulk cargo business was running out. Very few ships were built after 1895. The down turn in freight rates made it difficult for many local sailing ship owners to carry on. Ships were laid up for lack of cargo or sold to foreign flags. In this picture two three masted barques are seen laid up in the south corner of Georges Dock. It must have been in either 1897 or 1898 because the picture had been taken from the deck of a pilot steamer. These did not come into service until 1896/7 and the dock itself was closed in 1899. It is difficult to appreciate that these two vessels lie afloat on what today is the Mersey Docks and Harbour Company's office. In the background to the left of the ships there are other old buildings which have since disappeared. The tall ones are the salt warehouses of Nova Scotia and the building facing the quay is the Flatman's Mission at the bottom of Irwell Street.

Sailing ships did not vanish from the port overnight, but they were an increasingly rare sight by the 1920s.

The sketch shows the *Lawhill* off the Rock Lighthouse in 1926. This must have been about the last occasion that a large cargo carrying sailing ship came up the Mersey under her own sails. It seems that on this occasion the *Lawhill* arrived with a cargo of grain all the way from Australia to find there were no tugs available. As the wind was fair her skipper decided to sail from the Bar into the Mersey to anchor off Birkenhead to await the opening of the Alfred entrance gates.

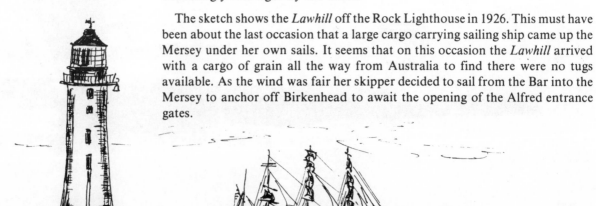

The *Lawhill* was one of the very few sailing ships that survived in the deep sea trades after the First World War. Most of the British owned vessels including the Liverpool ones had either been sold before the war or sunk during it. Those that were still afloat mainly flew the flags of Finland. The *Lawhill* was a British built four masted barque built in 1892. She was owned by Captain Barrie of Dundee and was involved in the jute trade between India and Dundee. In 1900 she was sold to the Anglo-American Oil Co. who used her to carry cargoes of oil and petrol in tins. They, in turn, sold her in 1911 to G. Windram and Co. of Liverpool for only £5500. At the outbreak of war Windrams quickly sold her at a profit to Finnish owners and she stayed with the Finnish flag until she was seized by the South African government in the Second World War. Her rusting hulk was still visible at Lourenco Marques until the 1960s.

The introduction of steam tugs to the Mersey in the 1820s made an enormous difference to the sailing ship fleet. Ships could be held up for weeks in the Mersey because of contrary winds. By employing a tug they could get clear of the dangerous confines of the river and out to the open sea. Quite often the first steam ferries on the river would act as tugs. This was often much to the annoyance of passengers since it disrupted the ferry service. In 1836 the first tug company was formed and this was shortly followed by a dozen others, all competing fiercely for the towage business in and out of the river.

The sight of a sailing ship coming into the Mersey under sail has not entirely been forgotten for there have been several occasions in the last fifteen years when the sail training ships like the schooners *Malcolm Miller* and *Sir Winston Churchill* have come in under sail. The arrival and departure of the sail training ships in the Tall Ships Race promises to be a special treat for everyone interested in sailing ships.

Pilot Boats

No.3 pilot schooner The Duke *was the second pilot schooner for the Liverpool service. Built by Buckley Jones of Liverpool in 1852, she had a long career and was finally sold to Danish owners for use as a fishing boat in 1894.*

The first organised pilot service on the Mersey started in 1766. The same service continues to this day. The boats have changed but the need for expert advice to enter and to leave our difficult river has not. The first pilot boats were cutters, about fifty feet long and painted in a distinctive way with large numbers on their sails. By the early 1800s there were about a dozen of them each carrying six or seven pilots, 3 apprentices who acted as crew and the pilot boat master. In fact there were usually two masters, one on duty and one on leave ashore. This meant that the boat could be kept out on station in the approaches to the river for as long as possible. The boats were stationed between the Mersey entrance and the north coast of Anglesey so that ships approaching the port of Liverpool had several opportunities to find a boat and collect a pilot.

Pilotage was a hazardous job. The most dangerous part was the transfer from the pilot boat's small rowing boat (called a punt) to the boarding ladder which was hung down the side of the ship. The accompanying sketch shows the ship *Sandbach* inward bound from the West Indies with a cargo of sugar and molasses picking up her pilot. She has the sails on her main mast (the middle one) backed. This means she is stationary and it is safe for the little rowing punt to run alongside. The pilot cutter number 10 was called the *Town of Liverpool*. She was built at Liverpool in 1835 by Thomas Royden at his shipyard in the South Docks. She was sold out of the service in 1854.

Number Ten was sold to make way for a new bigger type of pilot boat. They were the pilot schooners. The first, the *Pioneer* number 6 boat was built in Liverpool in 1852 and was followed by another five by 1856. They were built in several different places Cowes, Ipswich, Ramsey, Isle of Man and Amlwch on the North Wales coast. The next sketch shows Number 11 the *Mersey* ready for launching at William Thomas's shipyard in 1875. The last pilot schooner was the George Holt. Built in 1890 she was the biggest of them all — 101 feet long. That

was almost 20 feet longer than most of the earlier schooners. To be honest the day of the sailing pilot boat had gone already for in the previous decade at least half a dozen schooners had been sunk or damaged in collision with steamers. The pilots were reluctant to give up their tried and trusted craft for new fangled steamers. But they had to in the end. The first steamers came into service in 1896 and proved a great success and the schooners were sold. The George Holt was the last survivor and the accompanying photo shows a group of pilots on deck standing round her tiller. The Falklands Company bought her in 1904 and used her for collecting shipments of wool from the outlying farms. By 1933 she was downgraded to a lighter in Stanley harbour where she eventually sank at her moorings. So far as we can tell she still lies on the bottom — the last of the pilot schooners.

Pilots on board the pilot schooner George Holt.

George Holt, *last of sixty one pilot boats, was built at Dartmouth in 1892. She was sold for trading around the Falkland Islands in 1904.*

Mersey Flats

Flats were the sailing barges of the Mersey and the Weaver and the canals leading off the Mersey. As their name suggests they were flat bottomed and built to carry the maximum amount of cargo and not for speed. They were very strongly built and some lasted for over a century. They were steered by a huge rudder hung on the sternpost. The rig of the flat was developed in the first half of the 18th century. The sails were invariably tanned a deep brownish red which made a distinctive contribution to the river scene. The crew consisted of no more than two men and perhaps a boy. Flatmen were very knowledgeable about the tides, currents, mud flats and all the other natural hazards of the Mersey. They became expert at manoevring their bulky craft in and out of dock and up the tortuous channels of the upper Mersey. Quite a few sailed along the coast to the chemical works at Fleetwood and North Wales for example. At their peak there must have been more than three hundred flats sailing on the river. By 1900 many had been stripped of their sails and were towed by tugs.

Apart from one, most of the sailing flats seemed to have finished work by about 1930. The exception was the *Keskadale* which was owned by the sand and gravel merchants Abels of Widnes. She was frequently kept busy supplying sand dredged from the river for the building of the Otterspool promenade. When the wind was fair she would use her sails to move her cargo from the dredger. If the wind did not serve then she would be towed by a tug. She continued working until 1947. No sailing flat has been preserved. Unlike the Thames barges and the Humber keel and the Norfolk wherry which can all still be seen under sail in their

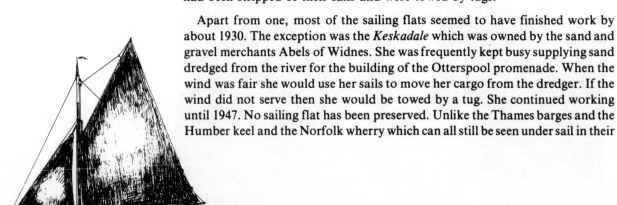

native waters it seems that there is no suitable hull left to restore and rerig. This is a pity. Perhaps a search of the backwaters of the Weaver — at Winsford Flashes for instance — might reveal a submerged hull in recoverable condition. The nearest is the *Mossdale* which is on show at the Boat Museum, Ellesmere Port. She has the same line as a sailing flat but she was always used as a dumb barge towed by a tug. Another intriguing possibility would be to build a replica of a flat. The information certainly exists but it would be an exceedingly expensive project.

The *Elvira* and the *Elissa*

The *Elvira* and the *Elissa* were a pair of identical twins, three masted iron barques. They came from the shipyard of Alexander Hall of Aberdeen in 1877. Halls were reckoned among the best shipbuilders of their time. The barque's owner was a Captain Henry Watt. He enjoyed a considerable inheritance and used some of it to buy his two ships. Sometimes he commanded them himself but more often than not employed other master mariners. He ran his shipowning business from his house in Wavertree and found plenty of time for other activities. He was a great hunting enthusiast. He was also a major figure in the Mercantile Marine Service Association in which he eventually became a vice president. He wrote frequently for their journal on all manner of subjects, anything from the work of Bidston Observatory to the poor quality of English seamen and the misguided legislation of Mr. Samuel Plimsoll, M.P. His rather casual and intermittent attention to his shipowning business caught up with him and he was obliged to sell his ships in 1896 and 1897. The *Elvira* has long disappeared though this photograph of her painting still survives in the Merseyside Maritime Museum. But the *Elissa* is still afloat and sailing!

After she was sold the *Elissa* passed through many different owners. Her rig was gradually reduced for the sake of economy and the second picture shows her as a barquentine under the Swedish flag about 1929. She was then known as *Fjeld* later she changed her name to *Gustav* and was still trading in the 1950s though by this time under power alone with no sails. It says something for the quality of her building that she lasted so long. In fact she continued trading, and by the late 1960s she was Greek owned and used for smuggling cigarettes from Yugoslavia to Italy. Then in 1969 she was considered too risky for this work — her profile was too easily recognised by the Customs authorities — she was ready for the scrapyard. Fortunately, an American archaeologist, Peter Throckmorton, recognised her for what she was, bought her in order to save her and eventually was able to interest the Galveston Historical Foundation to undertake her restoration. This was a long and arduous task. Many of her iron plates had to be replaced. A job that took a full two years. She was then towed back to Galveston, again after many crises and problems and there she was redecked and rerigged completely. Merseyside Maritime Museum contributed to this work because we found her original sail plan with all the vital dimensions in our plan collection. In 1982, the restoration was finished, she once again put to sea for short day cruises of the port of Galveston. She sailed again in 1983 on her 106th birthday and in 1984 it is intended to take her to New Orleans for the Louisiana World Exposition. It is good to know that at least one old Liverpool sailing barque is still sailing.

The barque rig became very popular in the 1870s because it saved on sails and crew with not too great a loss of speed. The second sketch shows the *Allonby*, another Liverpool barque of the same decade as the *Elvira* and *Elissa* sailing under topsails only.

Tern Schooners in Albert Dock

Albert Dock **not** in the heyday of sail! This photograph has an interesting story. The Albert Dock and its warehouses were first opened in 1846 and were intended as an unloading dock for valuable imports. The ships could discharge their cargoes directly into secure, fire proof storage. It was for deep sea sailing ships of about the 500 to 600 ton range. As the size of ships increased rapidly at the end of the 19th century the use of the Albert as an unloading berth declined. Instead, the warehouses received goods for storage from other docks in the port either by barge or by road. The water space was then largely turned over to ships without any work and this picture shows just such a situation. It was about 1919 or 1920 after the end of the First World War. Four three masted schooners — three with white hulls and one with a black hull up against the warehouse overshadowed by the others. The black one has not been identified but the others are, from left to right, the *E.H. Wharton Davies,* the *Adam B. Mackay* and the Alfred Ock Hedley. All three were built at Shelburne in Nova Scotia on the east coast of Canada in 1917. There was a terrible shortage of ships at that time because of the vessels sunk by the German submarines, and building wooden sailing and steam ships enjoyed a short lived revival in Canada as part of the effort to build a replacement fleet. These particular schooners were brought to Liverpool for the West African trade because there were not sufficient steamers. The three 'terns', as the Canadian schooners were called, filled the gap. But after the end of the war there was soon a surplus of all kinds of ships and they were quickly laid up and then sold away from Liverpool. They must have been about the last big sailing ships to be owned in the port.

The Nobby

The nobby is the main type of inshore fishing boat in and around the Mersey. There are still quite a number afloat though most of them are fitted with engines. Some still carry sails and in the 1982 River Festival there was a special race for them. I hope this revival of interest in this splendid design of local boat continues.

The nobbies or prawners as they are known in some places were designed for trawling in inshore waters. Their powerful cutter rig gave them the power to pull a large beam trawl and deliver their catches to market quickly. Their present design appears to have been developed in the 1890s. The earlier boats had straight stems and transom sterns whereas the nobbies have a very rounded forefoot and a graceful counter stern. It is likely that the hull shape was designed from late Victorian yacht designs. Whatever its origin the nobby proved to be an extremely popular boat, and was used by local inshore fishermen all along the north west coast from Cumbria to North Wales. Most of them were built at two boatyards — Crossfields of Arnside on Morecambe Bay and Crossfields of Conway. A few were also built at Marshside near Southport and probably a few on the Mersey. The oldest surviving nobby is the *Daystar* which is believed to have been built in 1894 at Arnside. She is being restored by the Merseyside Maritime Museum.

The nobbies' main catch at the right season of the year was shrimps. A huge shrimp catching and shrimp potting industry grew up at Southport were there was ready demand from summer visitors. Before the First World War there were up to one hundred small boats working from Southport. The fishery subsequently went into a deep decline as the local channels silted up. There were also nobbies based at New Brighton and Hoylake and in the Cockle Hole in the South Docks. They were even to be found as far up river as Runcorn and Widnes. A number of the survivors have been turned into yachts and sold away from the Mersey. Converted nobbies like the *Venture* which is based in the South West of England have done very well when racing against other vintage boats in the races organised by the Old Gaffers Association.

Steam and Sail

This photograph shows a transatlantic liner, possibly of the Allan Line, off Waterloo Dock. The remarkable thing about her is just how much sail she carried. Steam had been around on the Mersey from about 1815 first for small ships such as ferries and tugs and then by the late 1830s for Atlantic liners. The early liners were paddle propelled and the most succesful company the Cunard Line, had a substantial revenue from their contract to carry the mails across the Atlantic. The engines of these first liners used a lot of coal and there was little space left for paying cargo. Sails were retained as a means of economising on coal and on long voyages, such as that to Australia, the few steamers employed — the *Great Britain* for example — used their engines only in calms or contrary winds, relying for their main propulsion on their full set of sails.

The fuel economy of steamers gradually improved. One notable breakthrough was the development of a practical compound engine which used the steam twice. This was in large part due to the Liverpool engineer and shipowner Alfred Holt. With compound engines and higher boiler pressures Holt was able to design a ship capable of steaming 8000 miles without refuelling. He was able to start a steamer service to China from Liverpool with three ships fitted with his compound engines. They competed directly with the sailing ships which had hitherto had a monopoly of this valuable trade. The opening of the Suez canal in 1869 and the setting up of more coaling depots gave the steamer a growing advantage over the sailing ship. All the same sailing ships continued to be built and employed but for the bulk trades, coal, iron, nitrates, timber and grain. These were often loaded or delivered to far away ports with few cargo handling facilites. It often took weeks or even months to load and that was too long to keep an expensive steam ship tied up.

Many steamers still carried sails even though they had compound or the later triple expansion engines. This was partly for economy, partly from conservatism, for most shipmasters had been trained in sail, and partly as an insurance policy. On long ocean voyages sail could be useful if the engines or the single propellor were damaged. The sailing steamers gradually began to fade out in the 1880s and 1890s. None of the new Cunard or White Star ships of this period carried sails, but some of the more conservative companies continued a policy of sails. Thomas and John Brocklebank, the oldest firm in Liverpool shipowning, began to change from sail to steam in 1889 and even their third steamer, the *Pindari* of 1891 still carried a set of sails as I have shown in the accompanying sketch.

The *De Wadden* at Widnes Bank Dock

The *De Wadden* was one of the last commercial sailing ships to trade into the Mersey. By the time this photograph was taken in the late 1950s she was really a motor ship with auxiliary sails. The engine was kept running all the time and the sails assisted her in fair winds.

The *De Wadden* was built in Holland in 1917 where she was one of a new class of sailing ships — all fitted with diesel engines — developed by the Dutch. As a neutral country in the First World War the Netherlands was able to trade profitably both worldwide and coastwise. The profits made from the local wooden sailing barges became so great that it became possible for their family owners to buy new ships. Many bought ships like the *De Wadden* built of steel instead of wood and with a large diesel engine to assist when there was no wind. By the end of the war the diesel engine which was still something of a novelty and regarded by many as a bit unreliable had been developed and improved by the Dutch so that is was possible to build full powered coasters without any sails. These Dutch motor coasters provided formidable competition to the British coasters (still largely powered by steam) in the 1920s and 1930s. The *De Wadden* was sold by her Dutch owners in 1922, probably as a result of the development of the full diesel powered coasters and was bought by the Hall family of Arklow in the Republic of Ireland. She traded extensively around the Irish Sea and was often to be seen in the Mersey, especially at Garston and Widnes. In this particular picture she is at Widnes Dock unloading a cargo of pit props from Ireland. She would probably load a return cargo of coal. Widnes Dock is no more. It was filled in in the early 1970s, but the *De Wadden* still survives. After she finished trading in 1960 she was bought for use as a cruise vessel, a yacht. A later owner used her both for excursions and also for collecting cargoes of sand for his building business. At present she is lying at Dunoon on the Clyde, but it is hoped that she will be preserved and that she will in fact return to the Mersey.

Topsail Schooner *Creek Fisher* ashore

at Blundellsands, 1904

The approaches to the Mersey were always dangerous for sailing ships and many have been blown ashore and wrecked. This is why Liverpool Bay was the first coast to have a lifeboat. A recent piece of research has shown that the Formby lifeboat station was set up some time in the early 1770s, about ten years before Bamburgh and that has always been recognised as the first. By the mid 19th century a whole network of lifeboat stations, including one at the Landing Stage at Liverpool, had been set up on both sides of the Mersey. They were run by the dock authorities until they were handed over to the Royal National Lifeboat Institution in 1894. The latter body already had one Mersey station at New Brighton. The pioneer station at Formby was closed in 1918, but the foundations of the old lifeboat shed can still be seen on the shore at Formby Point.

Like many another sailing ship caught in a vicious north west gale the *Creek Fisher* had dragged her anchors and went ashore. Her crew were all saved and she was refloated. Many ships were not so lucky and you will still find fragments of their timbers cast up on this coast from time to time. She was one of the best examples of the latter day coasting schooners. This was because she was made of iron rather than wood and also she was built by that master builder Paul Rodgers of Carrickfergus. Fortunately one of his ships — the schooner *Result* which was very similar to the *Creek Fisher* — has survived and is being preserved by the Ulster Folk and Transport Museum. The *Creek Fisher* belonged to the famous shipowning firm of Fishers of Barrow in Furness. By the end of the last century Fishers probably owned the biggest fleet of coasting schooners anywhere in the country. Early on in the 20th century they realised the days of sail were numbered and sold off their fleet and re-equipped with powered ships. Today they are still in business with a fleet of modern motor ships some of which can be seen in the Mersey from time to time.

Hoylake Trawlers in Albert Dock

Liverpool was never a major fishing port. But it has always had some fishermen. The great local centre for fishing in the 19th century was Hoylake. The Hoyle Lake had been the most important anchorage to the approaches to the Mersey in the 18th century. Ships could ride there safely to await a favourable wind to sail up the Rock Channel into the Mersey or perhaps to unload part of their cargo into barges. The village of Hoylake grew up alongside the anchorage to serve its needs. In the 19th century the Hoyle Lake decreased in importance largely because of the discovery of a new deep channel to the Mersey and to the increasing shallowness of the 'Lake' itself. It became the base for a fleet of large sailing trawlers. By 1872 there were thirty five of these Hoylake trawlers on the Liverpool Register. They ranged between 35 and 40 tons and in some cases were up to 70 feet long. They were almost all ketch rigged just as the boat in the picture. They were built in a wide variety of places including the Isle of Man, Whitehaven and Fleetwood. One, the *Emblematic* was actually built in Sunderland.

They fished with trawl nets which were dragged across the sea bed. The mouth of the trawl was held open by a large wooden beam which could be up to 50 feet long. This, and the iron heads on each end of the beam plus the weight of the nets and the catch inside were hauled on board by the crew using a hand winch. What a backbreaking job that must have been! By the 1890s most boats had fitted steam capstans to haul up the net. It was still a hard life especially in the Winter. Each boat carried a crew of four men and a boy who was learning the business whilst also acting as general dogsbody and cook; all for a shilling a week. The boy could expect to go on a share basis after 3 years, like the rest of the crew. There was a total of $6\frac{1}{2}$ shares: $2\frac{1}{2}$ for the owner, who was usually the skipper, one each for the crew. Fishing trips lasted for up to a week. The main fishing grounds were in Liverpool Bay between the Mersey, the Isle of Man and Morecambe Bay. A second rich ground was discovered in the 1870s in Cardigan Bay. Fish caught included sole, cod, plaice, haddock and roker. Although the trawlers were based on Hoylake they would often deliver their catches to Liverpool to sell them at the town's Fish Market. After the setting up of an ice plant in the D block of the Albert Dock warehouses in the 1890s they were frequently to be seen in the Albert and adjacent Canning Docks. The 1890s also saw the introduction of steam trawlers to the Mersey with the result that the fortunes of the less efficient sailing trawlers declined. A few continued to fish in the 1920s and 1930s after being fitted with engines. About the very last was the *Mermaid* which was burnt at Hoylake and the *Robert and Elsie* which was hit by a bomb in Dukes Dock in the Second World War. Not much survives of the history of these splendid local boats although they are still remembered in Hoylake where the same fishing families survive. In 1976 the County Museum tried to salvage the hull of the trawler *Emblematic*. This Hoylake trawler had been driven ashore in the great storm of January 1883. It proved impossible to refloat her and so after stripping off all her rigging and equipment she was buried in the sea wall at Meols. This wall was rebuilt in 1976 when her remains were revealed. She was floated out and taken back to the Hoylake anchorage only to be broken up by another great gale before she could be brought ashore. Some small sections of her hull were collected and a measured survey made by the Museum before the remains of the last survivor of the once important Hoylake trawler fleet were broken up and dispersed.

The accompanying sketch shows one of these Hoylake trawlers under sail bound for the Mersey with her catch.

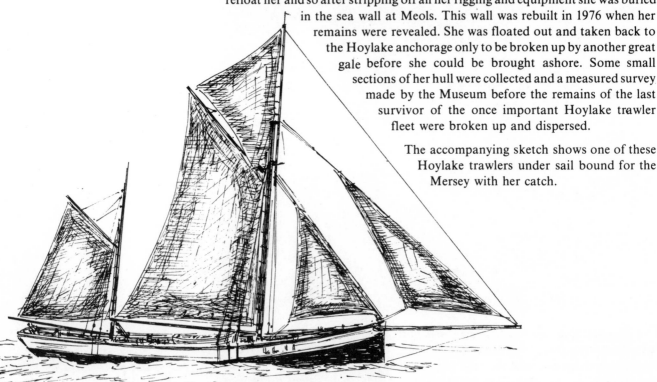

Coastal Vessels in Canning Docks, 1885

The key ketch *Windward* moves slowly to her berth at the South quay of Canning Dock under partly lowered fore staysail. Moving sailing ships around crowded docks called for fine judgement. Two cutters are unloading cargoes of stone onto the quay. They and the *Windward* are typical of the many small coasting craft that came to Liverpool with cargoes from the little ports of North Wales. Many of these ports were no more than a rocky inlet or a sandy beach close to a quarry. But because areas like the Lleyn peninsular were not served by railways these little vessels played an important role in the local economy delivering cargoes of stone, grain etc. to the bigger ports and bringing back cargoes of coal.

The imposing building in the background is the old Customs House which was built on the site of Liverpool's first dock. It was badly damaged in the Second World War and later demolished, a sad loss to Liverpool's architectural heritage.

Boys and their Boats

Love of the sea and sailing was learned from an early age by many Merseysiders. Many a lad went to sea as apprentice or cabin boy at twelve or maybe thirteen years old. Some later rose to the top of their calling, commanding the finest liners of the port.